sweet & sporty DIAPER COVERS

New moms will love seeing their precious babies dressed up in these creative diaper covers for boys and girls. The designs are so fast and easy, you'll want to crochet them for all the special babies in your life. Each pattern can be made in three sizes ranging from newborns up to 12 months.

LOOK FOR THE CAMERA in our instructions and watch our technique videos made just for you! **www.LeisureArts.com/6719**

LEISURE ARTS, INC. • Maumelle, Arkansas

baseball

EASY

SHOPPING LIST

Yarn (Medium Weight) MEDIUM 4

[5 ounces, 256 yards (141 grams, 234 meters) per skein]:

- ☐ Blue - 1 skein
- ☐ White - 7 yards (6.5 meters)
- ☐ Red - small amount

Crochet Hook

- ☐ Size J (6 mm) **or** size needed for gauge

Additional Supply

- ☐ Yarn needle

SIZE INFORMATION

Finished Measurements:

Size	**Waist**	**Rise** (from top of front to top of back)
0-3 Months	12½" (32 cm)	13" (33 cm)
3-6 Months	13¾" (35 cm)	15" (38 cm)
6-12 Months	15" (38 cm)	16½" (42 cm)

Size Note: We have printed the instructions for the sizes in different colors to make it easier for you to find:

- Size 0-3 months in Blue
- Size 3-6 months in Pink
- Size 6-12 months in Green

Instructions in Black apply to all sizes.

GAUGE INFORMATION

14 sc and 16 rows = 4" (10 cm)

Gauge Swatch: 4" (10 cm) square

With Blue, ch 15.

Row 1: Sc in second ch from hook and in each ch across: 14 sc.

Rows 2-16: Ch 1, turn; sc in each sc across.

Finish off.

STITCH GUIDE

SINGLE CROCHET 2 TOGETHER *(abbreviated sc2tog)*

Pull up a loop in each of next 2 sc, YO and draw through all 3 loops on hook **(counts as one sc)**.

BODY

With Blue and leaving a long end for sewing, ch 23{25-27}.

Row 1 (Right side)**:** Sc in second ch from hook and in each ch across: 22{24-26} sc.

Note: Loop a short piece of yarn around any stitch to mark Row 1 as **right** side.

Rows 2 thru 13{15-17}: Ch 1, turn; sc in each sc across.

Rows 14{16-18} thru 18{20-22} (Decrease rows)**:** Ch 1, turn; sc in first sc, sc2tog, sc in each sc across to last 3 sc, sc2tog, sc in last sc: 12{14-16} sc.

Rows 19{21-23} thru 30{36-40}: Ch 1, turn; sc in each sc across.

Rows 31{37-41} thru 35{41-45} (Increase rows)**:** Ch 1, turn; 2 sc in first sc, sc in each sc across to last sc, 2 sc in last sc: 22{24-26} sc.

Rows 36{42-46} thru 48{56-62}: Ch 1, turn; sc in each sc across.

Finish off leaving a long end for sewing.

Using long end and matching rows, use mattress stitch *(Figs. 5a & b, page 31)* to join first and last 13{15-17} rows together on each side.

TOP EDGING

Rnd 1: With **right** side facing, join White with sc in first sc on Body *(Figs. 4a & b, page 30)*; sc in each sc and in free loop of each beginning ch around *(Fig. 2b, page 30)*; join with slip st to first sc, finish off: 44{48-52} sc.

Rnd 2: With **right** side facing, join Red with sc in first sc; sc in each sc around; join with slip st to first sc, finish off.

LEG EDGING

Rnd 1: With **right** side facing, join White with sc at seam on Leg opening; sc evenly around; join with slip st to first sc, finish off.

Rnd 2: With **right** side facing, join Red with sc in first sc; sc in each sc around; join with slip st to first sc, finish off.

Repeat for second Leg.

BASEBALL

Rnd 1 (Right side)**:** With White, ch 2, 6 sc in second ch from hook; do **not** join, place marker.

Markers are used to help distinguish the beginning of each round being worked. Place a 2" (5 cm) scrap piece of yarn before the first stitch of each round, moving marker after each round is complete.

Rnd 2: 2 Sc in each sc around: 12 sc.

Rnd 3: (Sc in next sc, 2 sc in next sc) around: 18 sc.

Rnd 4: (Sc in next 2 sc, 2 sc in next sc) around: 24 sc.

Rnd 5: (Sc in next 3 sc, 2 sc in next sc) around; slip st in next sc, finish off leaving a long end for sewing: 30 sc.

Using photo as a guide, embroider stitching on Baseball using Red straight stitches forming "v's" *(Fig. 6, page 31)*.

Using photo as a guide for placement and long end, sew Baseball to Diaper Cover.

stripes

EASY

SHOPPING LIST

Yarn (Medium Weight) 4 MEDIUM

[6 ounces, 315 yards (170.1 grams, 288 meters) per skein]:

☐ Dark Blue - 1 skein

☐ Blue - 1 skein

☐ White - 1 skein

Crochet Hook

☐ Size J (6 mm)

or size needed for gauge

Additional Supply

☐ Yarn needle

SIZE INFORMATION

Finished Measurements:

Size	Waist	Rise (from top of front to top of back)
0-3 Months	12½" (32 cm)	13" (33 cm)
3-6 Months	13¾" (35 cm)	15½" (39.5 cm)
6-12 Months	15" (38 cm)	16½" (42 cm)

Size Note: We have printed the instructions for the sizes in different colors to make it easier for you to find:

- Size 0-3 months in Blue
- Size 3-6 months in Pink
- Size 6-12 months in Green

Instructions in Black apply to all sizes.

GAUGE INFORMATION

14 sc and 16 rows = 4" (10 cm)

Gauge Swatch: 4" (10 cm) square

With Dark Blue, ch 15.

Row 1: Sc in second ch from hook and in each ch across: 14 sc.

Rows 2-16: Ch 1, turn; sc in each sc across.

Finish off.

STITCH GUIDE

SINGLE CROCHET 2 TOGETHER *(abbreviated sc2tog)*

Pull up a loop in each of next 2 sc, YO and draw through all 3 loops on hook (counts as one sc).

BODY

With Dark Blue and leaving a long end for sewing, ch 23{25-27}.

Row 1 (Wrong side)**:** Sc in second ch from hook and in each ch across: 22{24-26} sc.

Note: Loop a short piece of yarn around the **back** of any stitch on Row 1 to mark **right** side.

Row 2: Ch 1, turn; sc in each sc across changing to White in last sc ***(Fig. 3a, page 30)***; do **not** cut unused colors.

Carry unused colors along the edge.

Row 3: Ch 1, turn; sc in each sc across changing to Blue in last sc.

Row 4: Ch 1, turn; sc in each sc across.

Row 5: Ch 1, turn; sc in each sc across changing to White in last sc.

Row 6: Ch 1, turn; sc in each sc across changing to Dark Blue in last sc.

Row 7: Ch 1, turn; sc in each sc across.

SIZE 0-3 MONTHS ONLY

Rows 8 thru 12: Repeat Rows 2-6 once.

Cut White and Blue.

Rows 13-15: Ch 1, turn; sc in each sc across.

SIZE 3-6 MONTHS ONLY

Rows 8-18: Repeat Rows 2-7 once, then repeat Rows 2-6 once **more**.

Cut White and Blue.

SIZE 6-12 MONTHS ONLY

Rows 8-19: Repeat Rows 2-7 twice.

Cut White and Blue.

ALL SIZES

Rows 16{19-20} thru 20{23-24} (Decrease rows)**:** Ch 1, turn; sc in first sc, sc2tog, sc in each sc across to last 3 sc, sc2tog, sc in last sc: 12{14-16} sc.

Rows 21{24-25} thru 32{39-42}: Ch 1, turn; sc in each sc across.

Rows 33{40-43} thru 37{44-47} (Increase rows)**:** Ch 1, turn; 2 sc in first sc, sc in each sc across to last sc, 2 sc in last sc: 22{24-26} sc.

SIZE 0-3 MONTHS ONLY

Rows 38-40: Ch 1, turn; sc in each sc across changing to White at end of last row.

Rows 41-50: Repeat Rows 3-7 once, then repeat Rows 2-6 once **more**.

SIZE 3-6 MONTHS ONLY

Change to White at end of last row.

Rows 45-60: Repeat Rows 3-7 once, then repeat Rows 2-7 once, then repeat Rows 2-6 once **more**.

SIZE 6-12 MONTHS ONLY

Row 48: Ch 1, turn; sc in each sc across changing to White in last sc.

Rows 49-64: Repeat Rows 3-7 once, then repeat Rows 2-7 once, then repeat Rows 2-6 once **more**.

ALL SIZES

Cut White and Blue.

Rows 51{61-65} and 52{62-66}: Ch 1, turn; sc in each sc across.

Finish off leaving a long end for sewing.

Using long end and matching rows, use mattress stitch ***(Figs. 5a & b, page 31)*** to join first and last 15{18-19} rows together on each side keeping carried strands on wrong side.

LEG EDGING

Rnd 1: With **right** side facing, join Dark Blue with sc at seam on Leg opening ***(Figs. 4a & b, page 30)***; sc evenly around; join with slip st to first sc.

Rnd 2: Ch 1, sc in each sc around; join with slip st to first sc, finish off.

Repeat for second Leg.

football

EASY

SHOPPING LIST

Yarn (Medium Weight) 4 MEDIUM

[6 ounces, 315 yards (170.1 grams, 288 meters) per skein]:

- ☐ White - 1 skein
- ☐ Brown - 30 yards (27.5 meters)

Crochet Hook

- ☐ Size J (6 mm)

  or size needed for gauge

Additional Supply

- ☐ Yarn needle

SIZE INFORMATION

Finished Measurements:

Size	**Waist**	**Rise** (from top of front to top of back)
0-3 Months	12½" (32 cm)	13" (33 cm)
3-6 Months	13¾" (35 cm)	15" (38 cm)
6-12 Months	15" (38 cm)	16½" (42 cm)

Size Note: We have printed the instructions for the sizes in different colors to make it easier for you to find:

- Size 0-3 months in Blue
- Size 3-6 months in Pink
- Size 6-12 months in Green

Instructions in Black apply to all sizes.

GAUGE INFORMATION

14 sc and 16 rows = 4" (10 cm)

14 Linked dc and 8 rows = 4" (10 cm)

Gauge Swatch: 4" (10 cm) square

With White, ch 15.

Row 1: Sc in second ch from hook and in each ch across: 14 sc.

Rows 2-16: Ch 1, turn; sc in each sc across.

Finish off.

STITCH GUIDE

SINGLE CROCHET 2 TOGETHER *(abbreviated sc2tog)*

Pull up a loop in each of next 2 sts, YO and draw through all 3 loops on hook **(counts as one sc)**.

LINKED DOUBLE CROCHET *(abbreviated Linked dc)*

Ch 3, insert hook in second ch from hook, YO and pull up a loop, skip next ch, insert hook in first st, YO and pull up a loop (3 loops on hook), (YO and draw through 2 loops on hook) twice **(first Linked dc made)**.

★ Insert hook in horizontal bar on last st made ***(Fig. A)***, YO and pull up a loop, insert hook in next st, YO and pull up a loop (3 loops on hook), (YO and draw through 2 loops on hook) twice **(Linked dc made)**; repeat from ★ for each Linked dc.

Fig. A

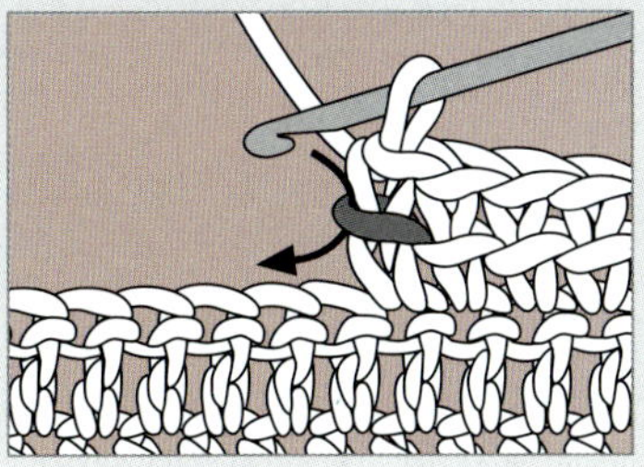

BODY

With White and leaving a long end for sewing, ch 23{25-27}.

Row 1 (Right side)**:** Sc in second ch from hook and in each ch across: 22{24-26} sc.

Note: Loop a short piece of yarn around any stitch to mark Row 1 as **right** side.

Rows 2 thru 7{8-9}: Turn; work Linked dc in each st across.

Rows 8{9-10} thru 12{13-14} (Decrease rows)**:** Ch 1, turn; sc in first st, sc2tog, sc in each st across to last 3 sts, sc2tog, sc in last st: 12{14-16} sc.

Rows 13{14-15} thru 24{29-32}: Ch 1, turn; sc in each sc across.

Rows 25{30-33} thru 29{34-37} (Increase rows)**:** Ch 1, turn; 2 sc in first sc, sc in each sc across to last sc, 2 sc in last sc: 22{24-26} sc.

Rows 30{35-38} thru 35{41-45}: Turn; work Linked dc in each st across.

Row 36{42-46}: Ch 1, turn; sc in each st across; finish off leaving a long end for sewing.

Using long end and matching rows, use mattress stitch ***(Figs. 5a & b, page 31)*** to join first and last 7{8-9} rows together on each side.

TOP EDGING

Rnd 1: With **right** side facing, join Brown with sc in first sc on Body ***(Figs. 4a & b, page 30)***; sc in each sc and in free loop of each beginning ch around ***(Fig. 2b, page 30)***; join with slip st to first sc: 44{48-52} sc.

Rnd 2: Ch 1, sc in each sc around; join with slip st to first sc, finish off.

LEG EDGING

Rnd 1: With **right** side facing, join Brown with sc at seam on Leg opening; sc evenly around; join with slip st to first sc.

Rnd 2: Ch 1, sc in each sc around; join with slip st to first sc, finish off.

Repeat for second Leg.

FOOTBALL

Row 1: With Brown, ch 2, 2 sc in second ch from hook.

Row 2: Ch 1, turn; 2 sc in each sc: 4 sc.

Row 3: Ch 1, turn; 2 sc in first sc, sc in next 2 sc, 2 sc in last sc: 6 sc.

Row 4: Ch 1, turn; 2 sc in first sc, sc in next 4 sc, 2 sc in last sc: 8 sc.

Row 5: Ch 1, turn; 2 sc in first sc, sc in next 6 sc, 2 sc in last sc changing to White in last sc made ***(Fig. 3a, page 30)***; do **not** cut Brown: 10 sc.

Row 6: Ch 1, turn; sc in each sc across.

Row 7: Ch 1, turn; sc in each sc across changing to Brown in last sc; cut White.

Row 8: Ch 1, turn; dc in first sc, sc in next 4 sc, 2 sc in next sc, sc in next 3 sc, dc in last sc: 11 sts.

Row 9: Ch 1, turn; dc in first dc, sc in each sc across to last dc, dc in last dc.

Row 10: Ch 1, turn; dc in first dc, sc in next 4 sc, 2 sc in next sc, sc in next 4 sc, dc in last dc: 12 sts.

Rows 11-13: Ch 1, turn; dc in first dc, sc in each sc across to last dc, dc in last dc.

Row 14: Ch 1, turn; dc in first dc, sc in next 4 sc, sc2tog, sc in next 4 sc, dc in last dc: 11 sts.

Row 15: Ch 1, turn; dc in first dc, sc in each sc across to last dc, dc in last dc.

Row 16: Ch 1, turn; dc in first dc, sc in next 4 sc, sc2tog, sc in next 3 sc, dc in last dc: 10 sts.

Row 17: Ch 1, turn; dc in first dc, sc in each sc across to last dc, dc in last dc changing to White ***(Fig. 3b, page 30)***; do **not** cut Brown.

Row 18: Ch 1, turn; sc in each st across.

Row 19: Ch 1, turn; sc in each sc across changing to Brown in last sc; cut White.

Row 20: Ch 1, turn; sc in first sc, sc2tog, sc in next 4 sc, sc2tog, sc in last sc: 8 sc.

Row 21: Ch 1, turn; sc in first sc, sc2tog, sc in next 2 sc, sc2tog, sc in last sc: 6 sc.

Row 22: Ch 1, turn; sc in first sc, sc2tog twice, sc in last sc: 4 sc.

Row 23: Ch 1, turn; beginning in first sc, sc2tog twice: 2 sc.

Row 24: Ch 1, turn; beginning in first sc, sc2tog.

Edging (Right side)**:** Do **not** turn; sc evenly spaced around entire Football; join with slip st to first sc, finish off leaving a long end for sewing.

Using photo as a guide, embroider lacing on Football using White straight stitches ***(Fig. 6, page 31)***.

Using photo as a guide for placement and long end, sew Football to Diaper Cover.

denim & pockets

EASY

SHOPPING LIST

Yarn (Medium Weight)

[5 ounces, 251 yards (142 grams, 230 meters) per skein]:

- ☐ Blue - 1 skein
- ☐ Gold - 40 yards (36.5 meters)

Crochet Hook

- ☐ Size J (6 mm)
  or size needed for gauge

Additional Supply

- ☐ Yarn needle

SIZE INFORMATION

Finished Measurements:

Size	Waist	Rise (from top of front to top of back)
0-3 Months	12½" (32 cm)	13" (33 cm)
3-6 Months	13¾" (35 cm)	15" (38 cm)
6-12 Months	15" (38 cm)	16½" (42 cm)

Size Note: We have printed the instructions for the sizes in different colors to make it easier for you to find:

- Size 0-3 months in Blue
- Size 3-6 months in Pink
- Size 6-12 months in Green

Instructions in Black apply to all sizes.

GAUGE INFORMATION

14 sc and 16 rows = 4" (10 cm)
In (sc, dc) pattern,
14 sts and 12 rows = 4" (10 cm)

Gauge Swatch: 4" (10 cm) square
With Blue, ch 15.

Row 1: Sc in second ch from hook and in each ch across: 14 sc.

Rows 2-16: Ch 1, turn; sc in each sc across.

Finish off.

STITCH GUIDE

SINGLE CROCHET 2 TOGETHER ***(abbreviated sc2tog)***

Pull up a loop in each of next 2 sts, YO and draw through all 3 loops on hook **(counts as one sc)**.

FRONT POST TREBLE CROCHET ***(abbreviated FPtr)***

YO twice, working in **front** of previous row, insert hook from **front** to **back** around post of st indicated ***(Fig. A)***, YO and pull up a loop (4 loops on hook), (YO and draw through 2 loops on hook) 3 times.

Fig. A

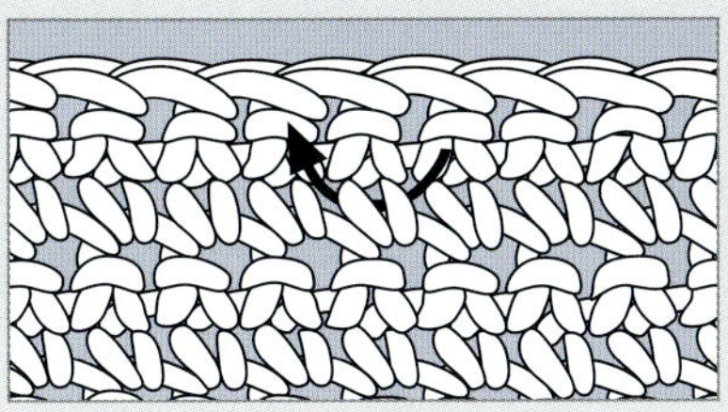

BODY

With Blue and leaving a long end for sewing, ch 23{25-27}.

Row 1 (Right side)**:** Sc in second ch from hook and in each ch across: 22{24-26} sc.

Note: Loop a short piece of yarn around any stitch to mark Row 1 as **right** side.

Rows 2 thru 11{12-14}: Ch 1, turn; sc in first st, dc in next st, (sc in next st, dc in next st) across.

Rows 12{13-15} thru 16{17-19} (Decrease rows)**:** Ch 1, turn; sc in first st, sc2tog, sc in each st across to last 3 sts, sc2tog, sc in last st: 12{14-16} sc.

Rows 17{18-20} thru 28{33-37}: Ch 1, turn; sc in each sc across.

Rows 29{34-38} thru 33{38-42} (Increase rows)**:** Ch 1, turn; 2 sc in first sc, sc in each sc across to last sc, 2 sc in last sc: 22{24-26} sc.

Rows 34{39-43} thru 43{49-55}: Ch 1, turn; sc in first st, (dc in next st, sc in next st) across.

Row 44{50-56}: Ch 1, turn; sc in each st across; finish off leaving a long end for sewing.

Using long end and matching rows, use mattress stitch ***(Figs. 5a & b, page 31)*** to join first and last 11{12-14} rows together on each side.

BELT LOOPS

Rnd 1: With **right** side facing, join Gold with sc in first sc on Body ***(Figs. 4a & b, page 30)***; sc in next 2 sc, work FPtr around st **below** next st, (sc in next 3 sts, work FPtr around st **below** next st) around working in sts and in free loop of each beginning ch ***(Fig. 2b, page 30)***; join with slip st to first sc, finish off: 44{48-52} sts.

LEG EDGING

Rnd 1: With **right** side facing, join Gold with sc at seam on Leg opening; sc evenly around; join with slip st to first sc, finish off.

Rnd 2: With **right** side facing, join Blue with sc in first sc; sc in each sc around; join with slip st to first sc, finish off.

Repeat for second Leg.

POCKET (Make 2)

With Gold and leaving a long end for sewing, ch 9.

Row 1 (Right side)**:** Sc in second ch from hook and in each ch across: 8 sc.

Row 2: Ch 1, turn; sc in each sc across.

Row 3: Ch 1, turn; sc in Back Loop Only of each sc across ***(Fig. 1, page 30)***.

Rows 4-6: Ch 1, turn; sc in both loops of each sc across.

Row 7: Ch 1, turn; beginning in first sc, sc2tog 4 times: 4 sc.

Row 8: Ch 1, turn; beginning in first sc, sc2tog twice: 2 sc.

Row 9: Ch 1, turn; beginning in first sc, sc2tog; finish off.

Using photo as a guide for placement and long end, sew Pockets to Diaper Cover.

mini skirt

EASY

SHOPPING LIST

Yarn (Medium Weight) 4

[5 ounces, 251 yards (142 grams, 230 meters) per skein]:

- ☐ Blue - 1 skein
- ☐ Pink - 1 skein

Crochet Hook

- ☐ Size J (6 mm) **or** size needed for gauge

Additional Supply

- ☐ Yarn needle

SIZE INFORMATION

Finished Measurements:

Size	**Waist**	**Rise** (from top of front to top of back)
0-3 Months	12½" (32 cm)	13" (33 cm)
3-6 Months	13¾" (35 cm)	15" (38 cm)
6-12 Months	15" (38 cm)	16½" (42 cm)

Size Note: We have printed the instructions for the sizes in different colors to make it easier for you to find:

- Size 0-3 months in Blue
- Size 3-6 months in Pink
- Size 6-12 months in Green

Instructions in Black apply to all sizes.

GAUGE INFORMATION

14 sc and 16 rows = 4" (10 cm)

14 dc and 8 rows = 4" (10 cm)

Gauge Swatch: 4" (10 cm) square

With Blue, ch 15.

Row 1: Sc in second ch from hook and in each ch across: 14 sc.

Rows 2-16: Ch 1, turn; sc in each sc across.

Finish off.

STITCH GUIDE

SINGLE CROCHET 2 TOGETHER ***(abbreviated sc2tog)***

Pull up a loop in each of next 2 sts, YO and draw through all 3 loops on hook (counts as one sc).

BODY

With Blue and leaving a long end for sewing, ch 23{25-27}.

Row 1 (Right side)**:** Sc in second ch from hook and in each ch across: 22{24-26} sc.

Note: Loop a short piece of yarn around any stitch to mark Row 1 as **right** side.

Row 2: Ch 1, turn; sc in each sc across.

Row 3: Ch 1, turn; sc in Back Loop Only of each sc across ***(Fig. 1, page 30)***.

Rows 4 thru 9{10-11}: Ch 2 **(does not count as a st, now and throughout)**, turn; dc in both loops of each st across.

Rows 10{11-12} thru 14{15-16} (Decrease rows)**:** Ch 1, turn; sc in first st, sc2tog, sc in each st across to last 3 sts, sc2tog, sc in last st: 12{14-16} sc.

Rows 15{16-17} thru 26{31-34}: Ch 1, turn; sc in each sc across.

Rows 27{32-35} thru 31{36-39} (Increase rows)**:** Ch 1, turn; 2 sc in first sc, sc in each sc across to last sc, 2 sc in last sc: 22{24-26} sc.

Rows 32{37-40} thru 37{43-47}: Ch 2, turn; dc in each st across.

Row 38{44-48}: Ch 1, turn; sc in each dc across.

Row 39{45-49}: Ch 1, turn; sc in Back Loop Only of each sc across.

Row 40{46-50}: Ch 1, turn; sc in both loops of each sc across; finish off leaving a long end for sewing.

Using long end and matching rows, use mattress stitch *(Figs. 5a & b, page 31)* to join first and last 9{10-11} rows together on each side.

LEG EDGING

Rnd 1: With **right** side facing, join Blue with sc at seam on Leg opening *(Figs. 4a & b, page 30)*; sc evenly around; join with slip st to first sc.

Rnd 2: Ch 1, sc in each sc around; join with slip st to first sc, finish off.

Repeat for second Leg.

SKIRT

Rnd 1: With **right** side facing, holding waist down, and working in free loops of sc on Row 2 and Row 38{44-48} *(Fig. 2a, page 30)*, join Pink with sc in first sc; sc in each st around increasing 8 sc evenly spaced; join with slip st to first sc: 52{56-60} sc.

Rnd 2: Ch 3 (**counts as first dc, now and throughout**), dc in next sc, ch 2, skip next 2 sc, ★ dc in next 2 sc, ch 2, skip next 2 sc; repeat from ★ around; join with slip st to first dc: 26{28-30} dc and 13{14-15} ch-2 sps.

Rnd 3: Ch 1, sc in first 2 dc, ch 2, skip next ch-2 sp, ★ sc in next 2 dc, ch 2, skip next ch-2 sp; repeat from ★ around; join with slip st to first sc.

Rnd 4: Ch 3, dc in next sc, ch 2, skip next ch-2 sp, ★ dc in next 2 sc, ch 2, skip next ch-2 sp; repeat from ★ around; join with slip st to first dc.

Rnds 5 thru 10{10-12}: Repeat Rnds 3 and 4, 3{3-4} times.

Rnd 11{11-13}: Slip st in next dc, 5 dc in next ch-2 sp, ★ skip next dc, slip st in next dc, 5 dc in next ch-2 sp; repeat from ★ around; join with slip st to first slip st, finish off.

ribbon ruffles

EASY +

SHOPPING LIST

Yarn

(Medium Weight) MEDIUM 4

[5 ounces, 256 yards

(141 grams, 234 meters) per skein]:

- ☐ Rose - 1 skein

(Ribbon, Super Bulky Weight) SUPER BULKY 6

[3.5 ounces, 42 yards

(100 grams, 38 meters) per skein]:

- ☐ 1 hank

Crochet Hook

- ☐ Size J (6 mm)
  or size needed for gauge

Additional Supply

- ☐ Yarn needle
- ☐ Sewing needle and matching thread

SIZE INFORMATION

Finished Measurements:

Size	Waist	Rise (from top of front to top of back)
0-3 Months	12½" (32 cm)	12½" (32 cm)
3-6 Months	13¾" (35 cm)	15½" (39.5 cm)
6-12 Months	15" (38 cm)	16" (40.5 cm)

Size Note: We have printed the instructions for the sizes in different colors to make it easier for you to find:

- Size 0-3 months in Blue
- Size 3-6 months in Pink
- Size 6-12 months in Green

Instructions in Black apply to all sizes.

GAUGE INFORMATION

14 sc and 16 rows = 4" (10 cm)

14 dc and 8 rows = 4" (10 cm)

Gauge Swatch: 4" (10 cm) square

With Rose, ch 15.

Row 1: Sc in second ch from hook and in each ch across: 14 sc.

Rows 2-16: Ch 1, turn; sc in each sc across.

Finish off.

STITCH GUIDE

SINGLE CROCHET 2 TOGETHER ***(abbreviated sc2tog)***

Pull up a loop in each of next 2 sts, YO and draw through all 3 loops on hook **(counts as one sc)**.

BODY

With Rose and leaving a long end for sewing, ch 23{25-27}.

Row 1 (Right side)**:** Sc in second ch from hook and in each ch across: 22{24-26} sc.

Note: Loop a short piece of yarn around any stitch to mark Row 1 as **right** side.

Row 2: Ch 1, turn; sc in each sc across.

Rows 3 thru 8{10-10}: Ch 2 **(does not count as a st, now and throughout)**, turn; dc in each st across.

Rows 9{11-11} thru 13{15-15} (Decrease rows)**:** Ch 1, turn; sc in first st, sc2tog, sc in each st across to last 3 sts, sc2tog, sc in last st: 12{14-16} sc.

Rows 14{16-16} thru 25{31-33}: Ch 1, turn; sc in each sc across.

Rows 26{32-34} thru 30{36-38} (Increase rows)**:** Ch 1, turn; 2 sc in first sc, sc in each sc across to last sc, 2 sc in last sc: 22{24-26} sc.

Row 31{37-39}: Ch 2, turn; dc in Back Loop Only of each st across *(Fig. 1, page 30)*.

Row 32{38-40}: Ch 1, turn; dc in both loops of each dc across.

Rows 33{39-41} thru 36{44-46}: Repeat last 2 rows, 2{3-3} times.

Row 37{45-47}: Ch 1, turn; sc in Back Loop Only of each dc across.

Row 38{46-48}: Ch 1, turn; sc in both loops of each sc across; finish off leaving a long end for sewing.

Using long end and matching rows, use mattress stitch ***(Figs. 5a & b, page 31)*** to join first and last 8{10-10} rows together on each side.

LEG EDGING

Rnd 1: With **right** side facing, join Rose with sc at seam on Leg opening *(Figs. 4a & b, page 30)*; sc evenly around; join with slip st to first sc.

Rnd 2: Ch 1, sc in each sc around; join with slip st to first sc, finish off.

Repeat for second Leg.

RUFFLE

Ribbon yarn may come in a hank. Unfold the hank and remove the thread ties. To make it easier to use, the Ribbon yarn may be wound evenly around an empty paper towel tube *(Fig. A)*. Place a rubber band around the Ribbon yarn on the tube to prevent it from unwrapping when not in use.

Fig. A

Ribbon yarn is made up of a band of loosely woven threads. The top edge has large loops that resemble a ladder. Crochet into these loops *(Fig. B)*.

Fig. B

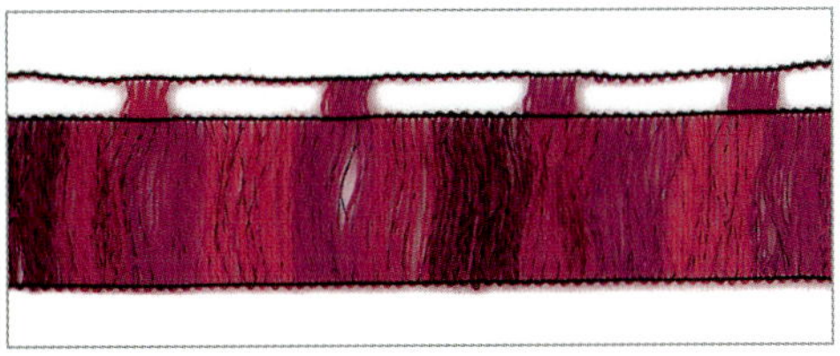

Hold the Body with **right** side facing and top edge down. Work Ruffle Row in free loops of Row 30{36-38} as follows *(Fig. 2a, page 30)*:

Ruffle Row: Insert hook in first sc, then through front to back of first and third hole on Ribbon yarn, draw both loops through sc *(Fig. C)*, ★ insert hook in next sc, then through first and third loop from hook on Ribbon yarn, draw both loops through sc and loop on hook; repeat from ★ across.

Fig. C

Cut Ribbon yarn leaving a short end. Using a sewing needle and matching thread, sew the remaining loop in place.

Repeat Ruffle Row working in free loops of each dc row.

crocodile ruffles

EASY +

SHOPPING LIST

Yarn (Medium Weight) MEDIUM 4

[5 ounces, 256 yards

(141 grams, 234 meters) per skein]:

☐ Purple - 1 skein

☐ Coral - 1 skein

Crochet Hook

☐ Size J (6 mm)

or size needed for gauge

Additional Supply

☐ Yarn needle

SIZE INFORMATION

Finished Measurements:

Size	Waist	Rise (from top of front to top of back)
0-3 Months	12½" (32 cm)	13½" (34.5 cm)
3-6 Months	13¾" (35 cm)	15½" (39.5 cm)
6-12 Months	15" (38 cm)	17" (43 cm)

Size Note: We have printed the instructions for the sizes in different colors to make it easier for you to find:

- Size 0-3 months in Blue
- Size 3-6 months in Pink
- Size 6-12 months in Green

Instructions in Black apply to all sizes.

GAUGE INFORMATION

14 sc and 16 rows = 4" (10 cm)

14 dc and 8 rows = 4" (10 cm)

Gauge Swatch: 4" (10 cm) square

With Purple, ch 15.

Row 1: Sc in second ch from hook and in each ch across: 14 sc.

Rows 2-16: Ch 1, turn; sc in each sc across.

Finish off.

STITCH GUIDE

SINGLE CROCHET 2 TOGETHER

(abbreviated sc2tog)

Pull up a loop in each of next 2 sts, YO and draw through all 3 loops on hook **(counts as one sc)**.

BODY

With Purple, ch 23{25-27}.

Row 1 (Right side)**:** Sc in second ch from hook and in each ch across: 22{24-26} sc.

Note: Loop a short piece of yarn around any stitch to mark Row 1 as **right** side.

Row 2: Ch 1, turn; sc in each sc across.

Rows 3 thru 9{10-11}: Ch 2 **(does not count as a st)**, turn; dc in each st across.

Rows 10{11-12} thru 14{15-16} (Decrease rows)**:** Ch 1, turn; sc in first st, sc2tog, sc in each st across to last 3 sts, sc2tog, sc in last st: 12{14-16} sc.

Rows 15{16-17} thru 26{31-34}: Ch 1, turn; sc in each sc across.

Rows 27{32-35} thru 31{36-39} (Increase rows)**:** Ch 1, turn; 2 sc in first sc, sc in each sc across to last sc, 2 sc in last sc: 22{24-26} sc.

Finish off.

CROCODILE STITCH

Size 0-3 Months & Size 6-12 Months ONLY

Row 1: With **wrong** side facing, join Coral with slip st in first sc on Body; ch 3 **(counts as first dc, now and throughout)**, dc in next sc, 2 dc in next sc, (skip next sc, 2 dc in next sc) across to last 3 sc, skip next sc, dc in last 2 sc: 22{26} dc.

Size 3-6 Months ONLY

Row 1: With **wrong** side facing, join Coral with slip st in first sc on Body; ch 3 **(counts as first dc, now and throughout)**, dc in same st, 2 dc in next sc, (skip next sc, 2 dc in next sc) across: 26 dc.

ALL SIZES

Row 2: Turn; slip st in first dc, skip next dc, work 4 dc down post of next dc ***(Fig. A)***, ch 1, rotate piece and work 4 dc up post of next dc to form a Scale ***(Fig. B)***, ★ skip next 2 dc, work 4 dc down post of next dc, ch 1, rotate piece and work 4 dc up post of next dc; repeat from ★ across to last 2 dc, skip next dc, slip st in last dc: 5{6-6} Scales.

Fig. A

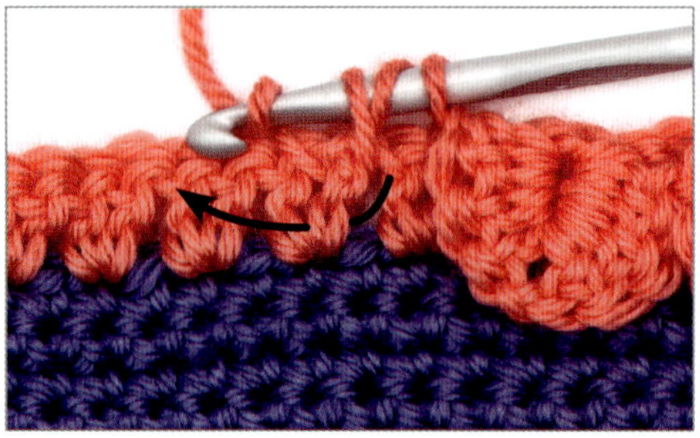

Fig. B

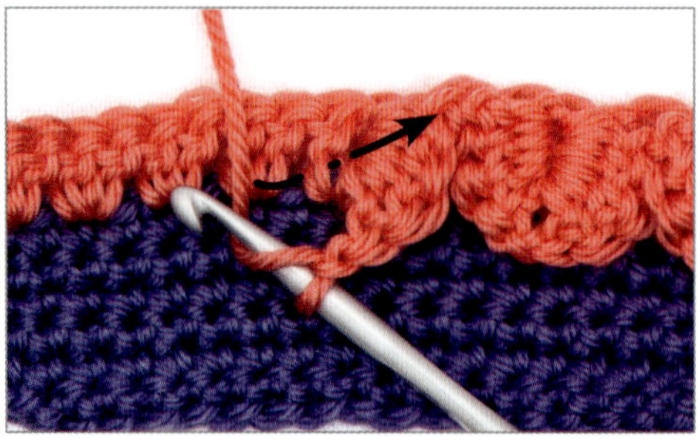

Row 3: Ch 3, turn; dc in same st, 2 dc in center of next Scale, ★ 2 dc in center of next 2-dc group working **around** previous row ***(Fig. C)***, 2 dc in center of next Scale; repeat from ★ across to last slip st, 2 dc in last slip st: 22{26-26} dc.

Fig. C

Row 4: Ch 3, turn; work 3 dc down post of first dc, ch 1, rotate piece and work 4 dc up post of next dc to form first Scale, ★ skip next 2 dc, work 4 dc down post of next dc, ch 1, rotate piece and work 4 dc up post of next dc; repeat from ★ across: 6{7-7} Scales.

Row 5: Ch 3, turn; dc in center of first Scale, ★ 2 dc in center of next 2-dc group working **around** previous row, 2 dc in center of next Scale; repeat from ★ across: 22{26-26} dc.

Size 0-3 Months ONLY

Rows 6-10: Repeat Rows 2-5 once, then repeat Row 2 once **more**; at end of Row 10, finish off.

Row 11: With **wrong** side facing, join Purple with slip st in first slip st; ch 1, 2 hdc in same st and in center of next Scale, ★ 2 hdc in center of next 2-dc group working **around** previous row, 2 hdc in center of next Scale; repeat from ★ across to last slip st, 2 hdc in last slip st; do **not** finish off: 22 hdc.

Size 3-6 Months ONLY

Rows 6-12: Repeat Rows 2-5 once, then repeat Rows 2-4 once **more**; at end of Row 12, finish off.

Row 13: With **wrong** side facing, join Purple with slip st in center of first Scale; ch 1, hdc in same sp, 2 hdc in center of next 2-dc group working **around** previous row, ★ 2 hdc in center of next Scale, 2 hdc in center of next 2-dc group working **around** previous row; repeat from ★ across to last Scale, hdc in center of last Scale; do **not** finish off: 24 hdc.

Size 6-12 Months ONLY

Rows 6-14: Repeat Rows 2-5 twice, then repeat Row 2 once **more**; at end of Row 14, finish off.

Row 15: With **wrong** side facing, join Purple with slip st in first slip st; ch 1, 2 hdc in same st and in center of next Scale, ★ 2 hdc in center of next 2-dc group working **around** previous row, 2 hdc in center of next Scale; repeat from ★ across to last slip st, 2 hdc in last slip st; do **not** finish off: 26 hdc.

TOP EDGE

Rows 1-3: Ch 1, turn; sc in each st across.

Finish off leaving a long end for sewing.

Using long end and matching rows, use mattress stitch ***(Figs. 5a & b, page 31)*** to join first 8{9-10} rows to Crocodile Stitch and last 3 rows.

LEG EDGING

Rnd 1: With **right** side facing, join Purple with sc at seam on Leg opening ***(Figs. 4a & b, page 30)***; sc evenly around; join with slip st to first sc.

Rnd 2: Ch 1, sc in each sc around; join with slip st to first sc, finish off.

Repeat for second Leg.

cupcake

EASY

SHOPPING LIST

Yarn (Medium Weight) MEDIUM 4

[3.5 ounces, 192 yards

(100 grams, 176 meters) per skein]:

☐ Variegated - 1 skein

[3.5 ounces, 205 yards

(100 grams, 187 meters) per skein]:

☐ Lavender - 1 skein

Crochet Hook

☐ Size J (6 mm)

or size needed for gauge

Additional Supply

☐ Yarn needle

SIZE INFORMATION

Finished Measurements:

Size	**Waist**	**Rise** (from top of front to top of back)
0-3 Months	12½" (32 cm)	13" (33 cm)
3-6 Months	13¾" (35 cm)	15" (38 cm)
6-12 Months	15" (38 cm)	16½" (42 cm)

Size Note: We have printed the instructions for the sizes in different colors to make it easier for you to find:

- Size 0-3 months in Blue
- Size 3-6 months in Pink
- Size 6-12 months in Green

Instructions in Black apply to all sizes.

GAUGE INFORMATION

14 sc and 16 rows = 4" (10 cm)

Gauge Swatch: 4" (10 cm) square

With Variegated, ch 15.

Row 1: Sc in second ch from hook and in each ch across: 14 sc.

Rows 2-16: Ch 1, turn; sc in each sc across.

Finish off.

STITCH GUIDE

SINGLE CROCHET 2 TOGETHER *(abbreviated sc2tog)*

Pull up a loop in each of next 2 sc, YO and draw through all 3 loops on hook (counts as one sc).

BODY

With Variegated and leaving a long end for sewing, ch 23{25-27}.

Row 1 (Right side)**:** Sc in second ch from hook and in each ch across: 22{24-26} sc.

Note: Loop a short piece of yarn around any stitch to mark Row 1 as **right** side.

Rows 2 thru 12{14-16}: Ch 1, turn; sc in each sc across.

Row 13{15-17}: Ch 1, turn; sc in each sc across changing to Lavender in last sc ***(Fig. 3a, page 30)***; cut Variegated.

Row 14{16-18} (Decrease row)**:** Ch 1, turn; working in Front Loops Only ***(Fig. 1, page 30)***, sc in first sc, sc2tog, sc in each sc across to last 3 sc, sc2tog, sc in last sc: 20{22-24} sc.

Rows 15{17-19} thru 18{20-22} (Decrease rows)**:** Ch 1, turn; working in both loops, sc in first sc, sc2tog, sc in each sc across to last 3 sc, sc2tog, sc in last sc: 12{14-16} sc.

Rows 19{21-23} thru 30{36-40}: Ch 1, turn; sc in each sc across.

Rows 31{37-41} thru 34{40-44} (Increase rows)**:** Ch 1, turn; 2 sc in first sc, sc in each sc across to last sc, 2 sc in last sc: 20{22-24} sc.

Row 35{41-45} (Increase row)**:** Ch 1, turn; 2 sc in first sc, sc in each sc across to last sc, 2 sc in last sc changing to Variegated in last sc; cut Lavender: 22{24-26} sc.

Row 36{42-46}: Ch 1, turn; sc in Front Loop Only of each sc across.

Rows 37{43-47} thru 48{56-62}: Ch 1, turn; sc in both loops of each sc across.

Finish off leaving a long end for sewing.

Using long end and matching rows, use mattress stitch ***(Figs. 5a & b, page 31)*** to join first and last 13{15-17} rows together on each side.

TOP EDGING

With **right** side facing, join Variegated with slip st in first sc on Body; working in sc on last row and in free loops of beginning ch ***(Fig. 2b, page 30)***, ★ skip next st, 5 dc in next st, skip next st, slip st in next st; repeat from ★ around working last slip st in joining slip st; finish off.

LEG EDGING

Rnd 1: With **right** side facing, join Lavender with sc at seam on Leg opening ***(Figs. 4a & b, page 30)***; sc evenly around; join with slip st to first sc.

Rnd 2: Ch 1, sc in each sc around; join with slip st to first sc, finish off.

Repeat for second Leg.

BODY RUFFLE

With **right** side facing, holding waist down, and working in free loops of Body ***(Fig. 2a, page 30)***, join Lavender with slip st in first st at side; ch 3, slip st in same st, (slip st, ch 3, slip st) in each st around; join with slip st to first slip st, finish off.

FLOWER

FRONT PETALS

Rnd 1: With Lavender, ch 2, 5 sc in second ch from hook; join with slip st to first sc.

Rnd 2: In each st around work (slip st, ch 1, 2 dc, ch 1, slip st); join with slip st to first slip st, finish off leaving a long end for sewing: 5 petals.

BACK PETALS

Rnd 1: With Lavender, ch 2, 7 sc in second ch from hook; join with slip st to first sc.

Rnd 2: In each st around work (slip st, ch 1, 3 dc, ch 1, slip st); join with slip st to first slip st, finish off: 7 petals.

Using photo as a guide for placement, sew Front Petals to center of Back Petals, then sew Flower to Body.

general instructions

ABBREVIATIONS

ch(s)	chain(s)
cm	centimeters
dc	double crochet(s)
FPtr	Front Post treble crochet(s)
hdc	half double crochet(s)
mm	millimeters
Rnd(s)	Round(s)
sc	single crochet(s)
sc2tog	single crochet 2 together
sp(s)	space(s)
st(s)	stitch(es)
YO	yarn over

SYMBOLS & TERMS

★ — work instructions following ★ as many **more** times as indicated in addition to the first time.

( ) or **[ ]** — work enclosed instructions **as many** times as specified by the number immediately following **or** work all enclosed instructions in the stitch or space indicated **or** contains explanatory remarks.

colon (:) — the number(s) given after a colon at the end of a row or round denote(s) the number of stitches or spaces you should have on that row or round.

GAUGE

Exact gauge is **essential** for proper size. Before beginning your project, make the sample swatch given in the individual instructions in the yarn and hook specified. After completing the swatch, measure it, counting your stitches and rows carefully. If your swatch is larger or smaller than specified, **make another, changing hook size to get the correct gauge.** Keep trying until you find the size hook that will give you the specified gauge.

CROCHET TERMINOLOGY		
UNITED STATES		INTERNATIONAL
slip stitch (slip st)	=	single crochet (sc)
single crochet (sc)	=	double crochet (dc)
half double crochet (hdc)	=	half treble crochet (htr)
double crochet (dc)	=	treble crochet (tr)
treble crochet (tr)	=	double treble crochet (dtr)
double treble crochet (dtr)	=	triple treble crochet (ttr)
triple treble crochet (tr tr)	=	quadruple treble crochet (qtr)
skip	=	miss

Yarn Weight Symbol & Names	LACE 0	SUPER FINE 1	FINE 2	LIGHT 3	MEDIUM 4	BULKY 5	SUPER BULKY 6	JUMBO 7
Type of Yarns in Category	Fingering, size 10 crochet thread	Sock, Fingering, Baby	Sport, Baby	DK, Light Worsted	Worsted, Afghan, Aran	Chunky, Craft, Rug	Super Bulky, Roving	Jumbo, Roving
Crochet Gauge* Ranges in Single Crochet to 4" (10 cm)	32-42 sts**	21-32 sts	16-20 sts	12-17 sts	11-14 sts	8-11 sts	6-9 sts	5 sts and fewer
Advised Hook Size Range	Steel*** 6 to 8, Regular hook B-1	B-1 to E-4	E-4 to 7	7 to I-9	I-9 to K-10½	K-10½ to M/N-13	M/N-13 to Q	Q and larger

*GUIDELINES ONLY: The chart above reflects the most commonly used gauges and hook sizes for specific yarn categories.

** Lace weight yarns are usually crocheted with larger hooks to create lacy openwork patterns. Accordingly, a gauge range is difficult to determine. Always follow the gauge stated in your pattern.

*** Steel crochet hooks are sized differently from regular hooks–the higher the number, the smaller the hook, which is the reverse of regular hook sizing.

CROCHET HOOKS																	
U.S.	B-1	C-2	D-3	E-4	F-5	G-6	7	H-8	I-9	J-10	K-10½	L-11	M/N-13	N/P-15	P/Q	Q	S
Metric - mm	2.25	2.75	3.25	3.5	3.75	4	4.5	5	5.5	6	6.5	8	9	10	15	16	19

BACK OR FRONT LOOP

Work only in loop(s) indicated by arrow ***(Fig. 1)***.

Fig. 1

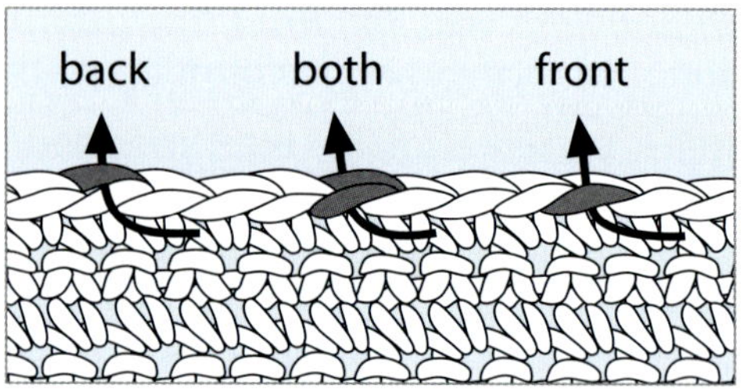

FREE LOOPS

After working in Back or Front Loops Only on a row or round, there will be a ridge of unused loops. These are called the free loops. Later, when instructed to work in the free loops of the same row or round, work in these loops ***(Fig. 2a)***.

Fig. 2a

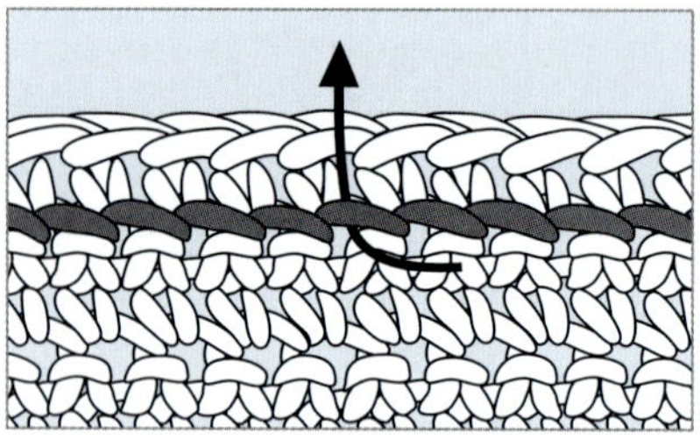

When instructed to work in free loops of a chain, work in loop indicated by arrow ***(Fig. 2b)***.

Fig. 2b

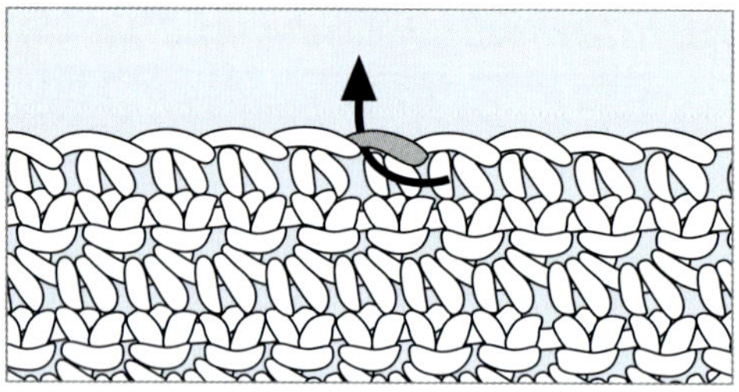

CHANGING COLORS

Work the last stitch to within one step of completion, hook new yarn ***(Fig. 3a or 3b)*** and draw through both loops on hook.

Fig. 3a

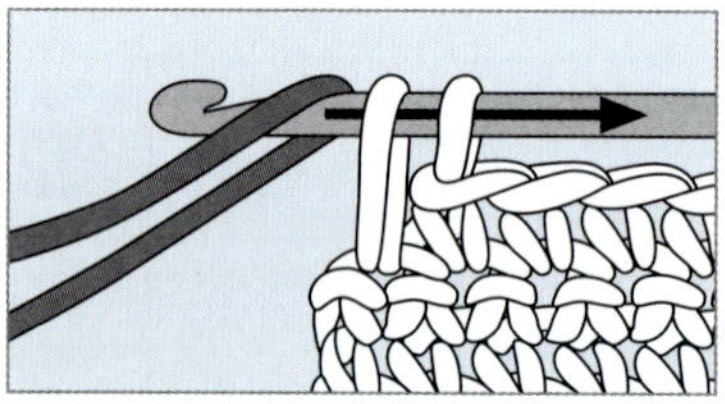

Fig. 3b

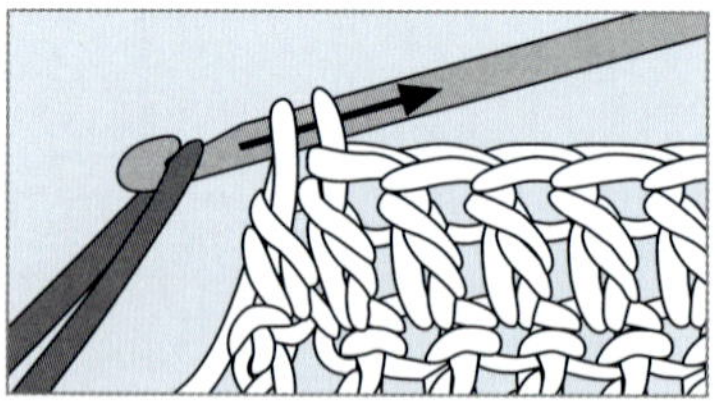

JOINING WITH SC

When instructed to join with sc, begin with a slip knot on hook. Insert hook in stitch indicated, YO and pull up a loop, YO and draw through both loops on hook ***(Figs. 4a & b)***.

Fig. 4a

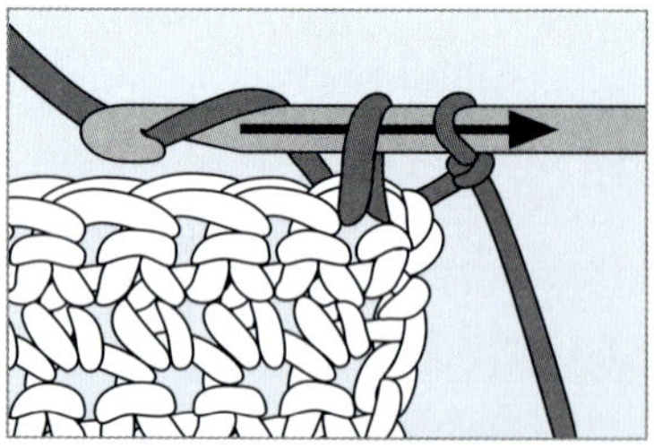

Fig. 4b

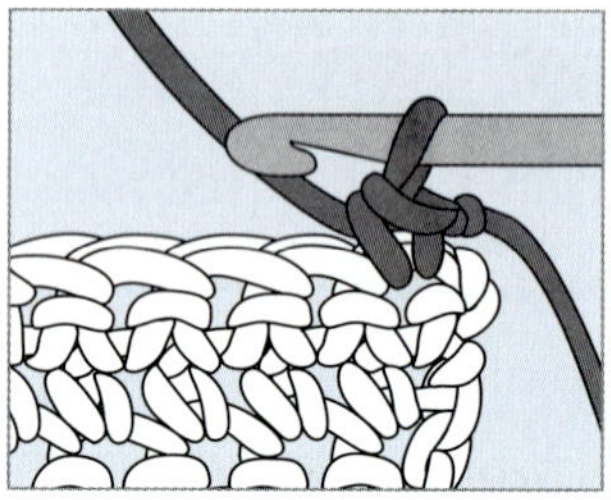

BEGINNER	Projects for first-time crocheters using basic stitches. Minimal shaping.
EASY	Projects using yarn with basic stitches, repetitive stitch patterns, simple color changes, and simple shaping and finishing.
INTERMEDIATE	Projects using a variety of techniques, such as basic lace patterns or color patterns, mid-level shaping and finishing.
EXPERIENCED	Projects with intricate stitch patterns, techniques and dimension, such as non-repeating patterns, multi-color techniques, fine threads, small hooks, detailed shaping and refined finishing.

MATTRESS STITCH

With the **right** side of both edges facing you and matching rows, sew through both sides once to secure the seam. Insert the needle from **back** to **front** through two strands on one side ***(Fig. 5a)***, then from **back** to **front** on the other side ***(Fig. 5b)***. Continue in this manner, drawing seam together as you work. This will create a flat seam.

Fig. 5a

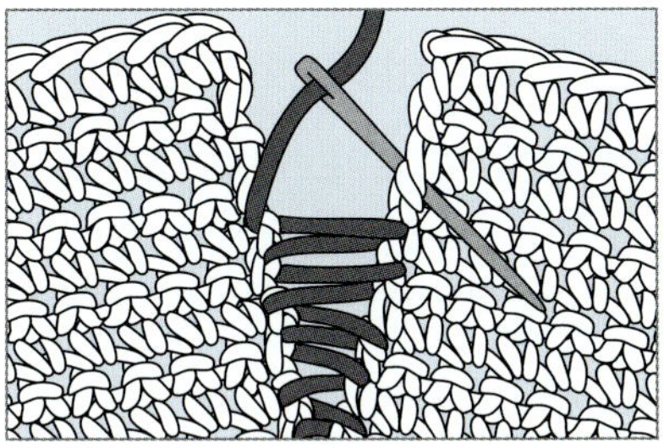

Fig. 5b

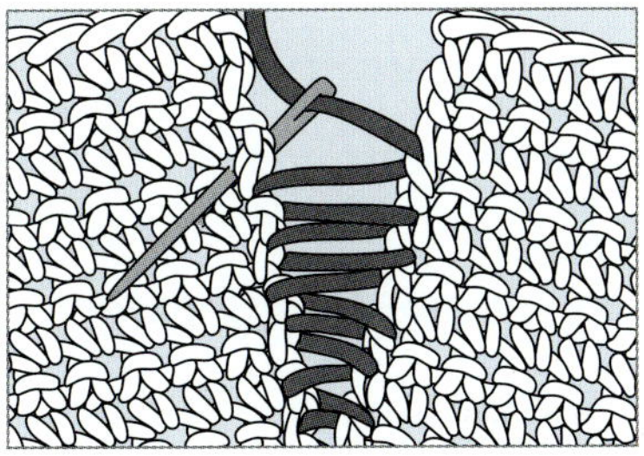

STRAIGHT STITCH

Straight Stitch is just what the name implies, a single, straight stitch. Come up at 1 and go down at 2 ***(Fig. 6)***.

Fig. 6

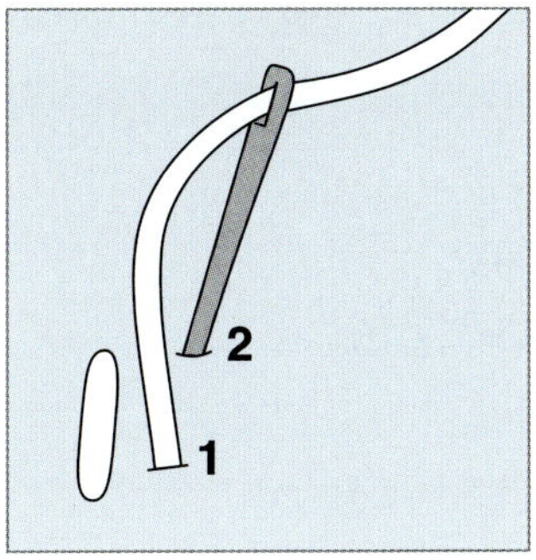

Meet the Designer: Kristi Simpson

Kristi Simpson enjoys designing cute baby gifts that mothers will love using. "There's just something special about having a handmade gift," she says. "It's personal and unique."

The mother of five says a diaper cover was actually one of her first designs. "Over the years, I have enjoyed changing the design and adding lots of unique touches."

Kristi became hooked on crochet after teaching herself so that she could help her daughter make a scarf from a "learn to crochet" kit that was a gift.

"I loved it from the beginning. I was amazed that I could take a string of yarn and create something so useful and pretty! Needless to say, I never stopped!"

Inspired by a love of yarn, Kristi enjoys creating crochet and knit patterns with a fresh and modern touch. Her designs have been published in several books and more than 50 magazine features. To see more of her designs, visit kristisimpson.net or find her on Ravelry, Facebook, and Pinterest.

yarn information

The Diaper Covers in this book were made using a variety of yarn weights. Any brand of the specified weight yarn may be used. It is best to refer to the yardage/meters when determining how many skeins or balls to purchase. Remember, to arrive at the finished size, it is the GAUGE/TENSION that is important, not the brand of yarn.

For your convenience, listed below are the yarns used to create our photography models. Because yarn manufacturers make frequent changes in their product lines, you may sometimes find it necessary to use a substitute yarn or to search for the discontinued product at alternate suppliers (locally or online).

BASEBALL

Red Heart® Soft®

Blue - #9851 Royal Blue

White - #4600 White

Red - #9925 Really Red

STRIPES

Caron® Simply Soft®

Dark Blue - #9710 Country Blue

Blue - #9709 Light Country Blue

White - #9701 White

FOOTBALL

Caron® Simply Soft®

White - #9701 White

Brown - #9750 Chocolate

DENIM & POCKETS

Lion Brand® Heartland®

Blue - #109 Olympic

Gold - #158 Yellowstone

MINI SKIRT

Lion Brand® Heartland®

Blue - #109 Olympic

Pink - #103 Denali

RIBBON RUFFLES

Red Heart® Soft®

Rose - #9779 Berry

Red Heart® Boutique Ribbons®

#1941 Rosebud

CROCODILE RUFFLES

Red Heart® Soft Baby Steps®

Purple - #9536 Light Grape

Red Heart® Soft®

Coral - #9251 Coral

CUPCAKE

Patons® Canadiana™

Variegated - #11420 Pretty Baby

Lavender - #10320 Cherished Lavender

We have made every effort to ensure that these instructions are accurate and complete. We cannot, however, be responsible for human error, typographical mistakes, or variations in individual work.

Production Team: Instructional/Technical Writer - Cathy Hardy; Editorial Writer - Susan Frantz Wiles; Senior Graphic Artist - Lora Puls; Photo Stylist - Sondra Daniel; and Photographer - Ken West.